South American Wildlife from A to Z

Animal Kingdom ABCs

A Photo Journey Exploring the Fascinating Creatures of South America with Fun Facts for Kids Who Love Wild Animals

by Michele Renee Acosta

Published by
Just Because...Books
an imprint of
My Extra Umbrella

South American Wildlife from A to Z:
A Photo Journey Exploring the Fascinating Creatures of South America
with Fun Facts for Kids Who Love Wild Animals
Copyright © 2025 by Michele Renee Acosta

Library of Congress Cataloging-in-Publication Data is available.
Library of Congress Control Number: 2024922757

ISBN (hardcover): 979-8-89615-063-3
ISBN (paperback): 979-8-89615-003-9
ISBN (ebook–Kindle edition): 979-8-89615-010-7
ISBN (ebook–EPUB edition): 979-8-89615-070-1

Published by
Just Because...Books
an imprint of My Extra Umbrella
1968 South Coast Highway
Suite 891
Laguna Beach, California 92651
Publisher@MyExtraUmbrella.com

This is Book 3 in the *Animal Kingdom ABCs* series.

Books in the *Animal Kingdom ABCs* series can be read in any order.

Printed in Laguna Beach, California, U.S.A.

First Edition

Author's Note

Welcome to *South American Wildlife from A to Z*, a book that invites young children to embark on an exciting adventure through South America's diverse wildlife. This book, part of the *Animal Kingdom ABCs* series, is designed to introduce children to wildlife from across the South American continent in a way that's both fun and engaging. While it may look like a traditional ABC book, it goes far beyond teaching the alphabet. Instead, it's a window into the fascinating world of the animals and other wildlife that inhabit this unique part of the globe.

Each book in the series is organized alphabetically, which helps young pre-readers easily follow along and engage with the content. However, it's not about "learning the ABCs" in the usual sense. Rather, it's about sparking curiosity about wildlife and showing how vast and varied the animal kingdom can be, one letter at a time. Many of the wildlife names in this book—like *vicuña* and *kinkajou*—are not words typically found in a traditional ABC book. That's part of the fun! While these words may be challenging to pronounce, it's a great way for children to expand their vocabulary and learn about creatures they might never have encountered before. Note that no wildlife exists in South America that begins with the letters Q or X. Rather than exclude letters from the alphabet, I've offered the opportunity for children to use what they've learned about wildlife from this part of the world to imagine an animal with features needed to survive in the habitats and climates on this continent.

Before reading for the first time, I encourage you to have a conversation about the animals children might expect to see in a book about South American wildlife. Ask children to share what they already know about animals in general and South American animals in particular. At the end of the book, you'll find fun facts about South American wildlife, as well as critical-thinking questions designed to inspire deeper conversations. These questions are perfect for further exploration of the topic and for encouraging curiosity and a life-long love of learning.

Remember, the goal of this book is discovery and wonder. It's okay if the animal names are tricky—that's why I included helpful pronunciations and facts! This book, and the series as a whole, aims to offer children an opportunity to explore the natural world continent by continent, fostering a sense of adventure, awe, and connection to the animals with which we share this planet.

Thank you for joining me on this exciting adventure through South America's animal kingdom!

Happy exploring!

Michele Renee Acosta

If you love *South American Wildlife from A to Z*, explore the rest of the *Animal Kingdom ABCs* series. Each book features real animals, surprising facts, and fun ways to spark curiosity. You'll also find other fiction and nonfiction series for children ages 3–8, along with a little something extra to download and enjoy.

A

Andean Condor

B

Black Caiman

C Capybara

D

Dolphin
(Amazon River)

E

Emperor Tamarin

F

Four-Eyed Fish

G

Giant Anteater

H

Howler Monkey

I

Iguana

J

Jaguar

K

Kinkajou

L

Llama

M

Maned Wolf

N

Nine-Banded
Armadillo

O

Ocelot

P

Pampas Cat

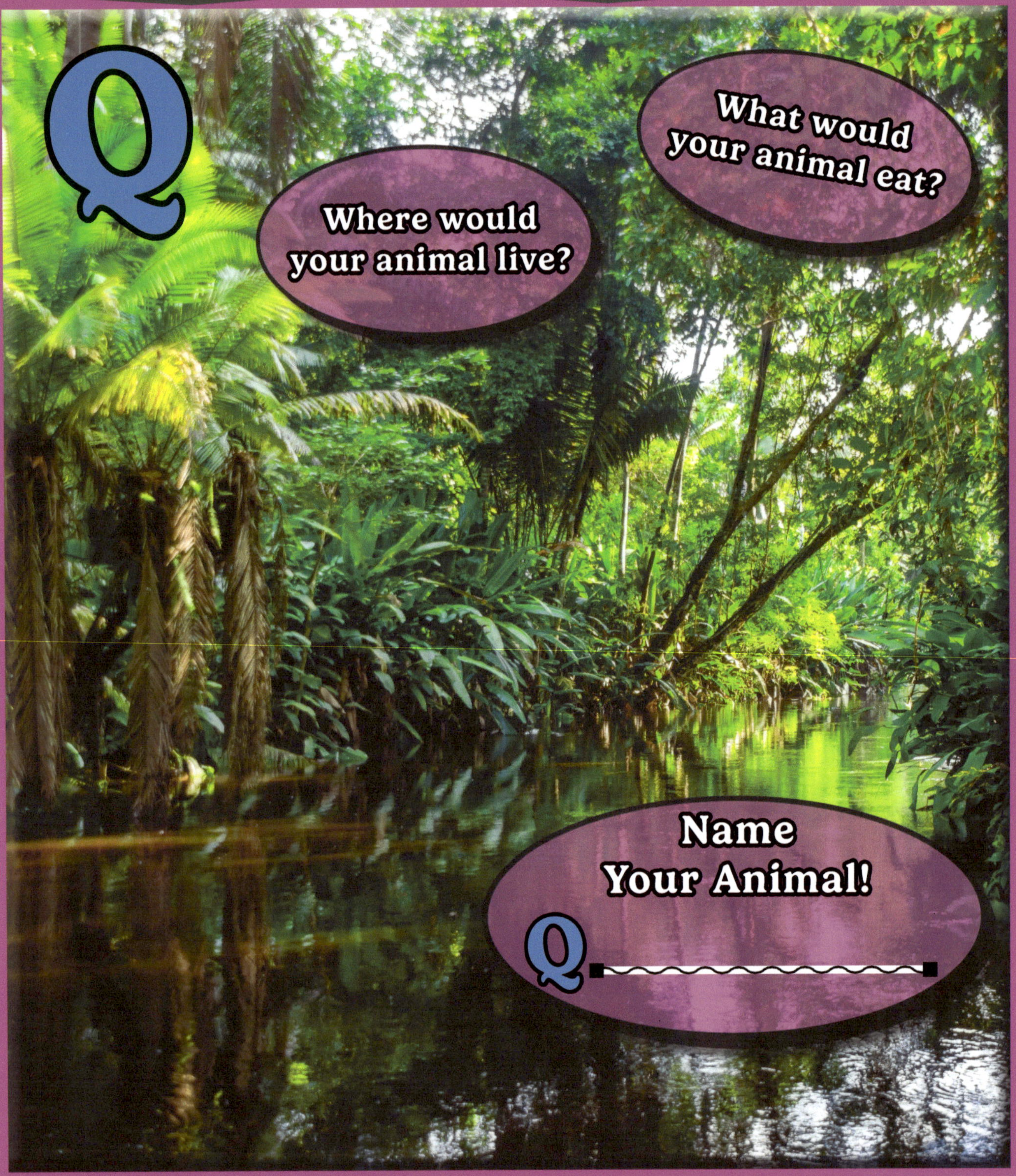

Invent an animal that could live in the Amazon Rainforest!

R

Red-Bellied Piranha

S

Sloth

T

Tapir

U

Uakari Monkey

V

Vicuña

W

White-Faced Saki

Where would your animal live?

What would your animal eat?

X

Name Your Animal!

X _____

Invent an animal that could live in the Andean Highlands!

Y

Yellow Anaconda

Z

Zebra Longwing
Butterfly

Would You Believe?

Andean Condors have one of the largest wingspans of any bird. It can stretch over 10 feet wide!

Black Caimans are the biggest crocodilians in the Amazon River basin and can even eat jaguars!

Capybaras are the world's largest rodents. They gather in large groups—sometimes over 100!

Amazon River Dolphins can turn their heads from side to side, unlike ocean dolphins.

Emperor Tamarins are named for their mustaches which look just like an emperor's mustache!

Four-Eyed Fish look like they have four eyes, but really they have two eyes split in half. One part sees above water and the other sees below!

Giant Anteaters have no teeth. But they can eat more than 30,000 ants and termites in one day.

Howler Monkeys are one of the loudest rainforest animals. They can be heard from 3 miles away!

Green Iguanas have a special "third eye" on top of their heads to help detect light and danger.

Jaguars have the strongest bite of any big cat and can crush bones with their jaws.

Kinkajous are also called honey bears. They have super long tongues to slurp up nectar.

Llamas can carry loads up steep mountains, but if you annoy them, they might spit!

Maned Wolves aren't really wolves. They belong in a special group all their own called *Chrysocyon*. (That's Greek for golden dog!)

Nine-Banded Armadillos can jump three to four feet straight up when scared!

Ocelots can climb, swim, and even sneak through the dark without making a sound!

Pampas Cats are named after the Pampas—a huge area of tall grasses in South America. Their fur helps them blend in with the tall grasses so they can sneak around without being seen!

Red-Bellied Piranhas are famous for their sharp teeth—but they mostly eat plants and insects!

Sloths are so slow that green algae grows in their fur, helping them hide in the trees.

Tapirs noses work like mini snorkels when they swim! You might spot a nose poking out of the water!

Uakari Monkeys have bright red faces. Scientists think the color shows how healthy they are!

Vicuñas are wild relatives of llamas. Their wool is one of the softest in the world.

White-Faced Sakis have a big fluffy tail and powerful jaws for cracking hard nuts.

Yellow Anacondas are great swimmers. They hide in water and wait for food to come close.

Zebra Longwing Butterflies sleep in groups at night, all cuddled together for safety!

What Do You Know?

Use these questions to spark curiosity and conversation. Talk about details you notice in the photos and what you've learned together from _Would You Believe?_ facts and other sources.

1. *Which South American animal surprised you the most? What about that animal is most interesting to you?*

2. *Which animal do you think would be easiest to spot in the wild? Which animal do you think would be hardest to spot? Why?*

3. *Which South American animal would you want to see up close? Why?*

4. *Which animals look like they might climb trees? What body parts do you think might help them climb?*

5. *Which animals do you think live in or near water? How do you think their body parts help them survive in their habitat?*

6. *Which animal has the biggest snout, or nose? What do you think it uses its nose for?*

7. *What do you think animals that live in the rain forest might have in common?*

8. *Which South American animals do you think live in groups? Which ones might live alone? What clues helped you decide?*

9. *Pick a South American animal. How do you think this animal protects itself from danger?*

10. *If you made up a new South American animal, where would it live and what would it eat?*

11. *Which animals do you think make loud sounds? Which animals might make quiet sounds?*

12. *If you could be one South American animal for a day, which animal would you choose? Why would you choose it?*

How Do You Say It?

Andean Condor (AN-dee-uhn KON-dor)

Black Caiman (BLAK KAY-muhn)

Capybara (KAP-ee-BAH-ruh)

Dolphin (Amazon River Dolphin)
  (DAHL-fin [AM-uh-zon RIV-er DAHL-fin])

Emperor Tamarin (EM-per-er TAM-uh-rin)

Four-Eyed Fish (FOR EYED FISH)

Giant Anteater (JY-uhnt ANT-ee-ter)

Howler Monkey (HOW-ler MUNG-kee)

Iguana (Green Iguana)
  (ih-GWAH-nuh ([GREEN ih-GWAH-nuh])

Jaguar (JAG-wahr)

Kinkajou (KING-kuh-joo)

Llama (LAH-muh)

Maned Wolf (MAYND WULF)

Nine-Banded Armadillo
  (NINE BAN-did ar-muh-DIL-oh)

Ocelot (OSS-uh-lot)

Pampas Cat (PAM-puhs KAT)

Red-Bellied Piranha
  (RED BEL-eed puh-RAHN-uh)

Sloth (SLAWTH)

Tapir (Lowland Tapir)
  (TAY-peer [LOH-luhnd TAY-peer])

Uakari Monkey (wuh-KAR-ee MUNG-kee)

Vicuña (vih-KOON-yuh)

White-Faced Saki (WYT-FAYST SAH-kee)

Yellow Anaconda (YEL-oh an-uh-KON-duh)

Zebra Longwing Butterfly
  (ZEE-bruh LONG-wing BUT-er-fly)

Sources BBC Earth (https://www.bbcearth.com); IUCN Red List of Threatened Species (https://www.iucnredlist.org); Mammal Diversity Database (https://www.mammaldiversity.org); National Geographic Kids (https://kids.nationalgeographic.com); National Wildlife Federation (https://www.nwf.org); NatureServe Explorer (https://explorer.natureserve.org); Panthera (https://www.panthera.org); Rainforest Alliance (https://www.rainforest-alliance.org); San Diego Zoo Kids (https://kids.sandiegozoo.org); Science News for Students: Four-Eyed Fish See Above and Below Water (https://www.snexplores.org); Smithsonian National Zoo & Conservation Biology Institute: Animal Index (https://nationalzoo.si.edu/animals); Smithsonian Tropical Research Institute: Zebra Longwing Butterfly (https://stri.si.edu); Wild Cat Conservation Alliance: Pampas Cat (https://wildcatconservation.org); World Wildlife Fund: Species Directory (https://www.worldwildlife.org/species)

More animals.
More fun.
More to explore.

www.ingramcontent.com/pod-product-compliance
Lightning Source LLC
Chambersburg PA
CBHW041545260326
41914CB00015B/1553